LIVING LEADERSHIP

by

Thomas Smith

ISBN-13: 978-0692249659 (Alternate Publishing)

ISBN-10: 0692249656

DEDICATION

This book is dedicated to Joshua Smith for his encouragement and support. A quotation that he shared with me has become one of my favorites.

"Don't be afraid to fail. Be afraid not to try." ~ Michael Jordan.

CONTENTS

PREFACE

"Living Leadership" is a motivational and career oriented business book that provides new insights into being better leaders. The collection of provocative essays provides perspective and understanding that are relevant for today's leaders. Written with the intention for leaders to help leaders, this book takes an unorthodox look at leadership. Inside perspective and practical tips are delivered and are meaningful to those interested in being better leaders. The book is especially relevant to those working with community groups, non-profits, and to improve individual skills and knowledge. This book provides useful information about critical leadership skills. Everyone has the opportunity to be leaders each and every day. This book helps to understand leadership and our ability to become better leaders. Today leadership takes many different forms. This book helps leaders to be able to envision the future and to convince others that they have the ability and vision worth following. After many years working in community organizations, the author's lessons learned and practical tips are shared so that the reader is able to become a better leader.

"You do what you think is best and the best that you can do. Not all agree and not all support... but you forge ahead with hope that there will be those that do get it and support your directions and path that you are trying to carve out." ~Thomas Smith

"To do a greater good – compromise may be required. Wisdom teaches us to value

friendship and cherish it." ~Thomas Smith

These characteristics help to make leaders successful.

Selflessness...Knowledge...Skill...

Implacability...Determination...

Perspective...Integrity...Focus...

Humility...Guidance...Fortitude...

Passion...Understanding...Patience...

Compassion...Enlightenment...

Decisiveness...Diplomacy...

Generosity...Listening Skills...

Consistency...Empathy...

Inspiration...Motivation...Respect...

Character...Charisma...Perspective...

Common Sense...Flexibility...

Objectivity...Detachment...

Responsibility...Perceptive...

Honesty...Insight...Adaptability...

Awareness...Humor...Commitment...

Communication...Lead By Example...

Vision...Enthusiasm...Tolerance...

Wisdom...Moral introspection...

Collaborative skills...

Strength...Thick Skin...Success...

Honor...Awareness...Compromise...

Creativity...Fairness...

Accountability...Patience...

Dedication...Diplomacy...

Loyalty...Unifying...Bodacious

Helpful...Efficient...Modesty...

Challenging...Transparent...

Responsible...Accessible...

Energetic...

and Having Good Judgement!

"Leaders are not born that way...they are developed through their experiences and their internal work. What good is an opinion where you don't have a responsibility? Leadership is practiced in attitude and actions...and results in inspiring achievement. Don't take yourself too seriously but do take your work seriously." ~ Thomas Smith.

VISIONARY LEADERSHIP

Leaders do not shirk from the overwhelming complexity of the world; instead they engage society with its competing, divergent viewpoints. In order to marshal the best possible chance of success, they seek to communicate effectively: sharing and listening, building their knowledge through collaboration.

* Being a leader or visionary of ideas requires passion about what you do.

* Being a leader or visionary of

ideas requires belief in yourself and your activity, product or service.

* Being a leader or visionary of ideas requires creativity and long-term planning.

Mahatma Gandhi did more than recognize the value of religious tolerance and sovereignty for the people of India; he used his life to make it possible. Gandhi drew on everything to instigate the changes he was seeking: his diet, his clothing, his community, his speech. When a reporter asked him to state his message for the world, Gandhi replied, "My life is my message."

Martin Luther King Jr. did more

than have a dream of racial equality in the United States; he advanced civil rights through a critical juncture in American history.

Among the qualities visionary leaders cultivate are imagination, engagement, tangible results, and penetrating self-reflection. A strong imagination is needed to envision the future with clarity. This makes it possible for all who share the dreaming to know the courses of action to be taken.

What is really needed today are visionaries who have explored new routes and new ideas and then are willing to serve as leaders. They have to courageously communicate the vision to others. The world needs leaders who act altruistically from a higher vision and from a deeper spiritual motive of service—and then carry it through.

ORGANIZATIONAL SUSTAINABILITY

No organization is sustainable if the membership or stakeholders are not cohesive. Respect and appreciation for each other make the whole stronger than its individual parts. It is essential that the leadership invest time in building a sense of team among the members. This can be accomplished in many different ways.

Each individual person should be encouraged to understand how he/she contributes to the whole. Further, each leader should be encouraged to learn how the others contribute. Attend each other's events. Shadow each other at events or in the planning sessions to gain a healthy respect for each other's expertise. Finally, plan a few events/parties each year that build cohesion and team among the whole group. Shut the organizations' *work* and go bowling together, have dinner and plan to talk about cutting-edge issues. These are healthy investments in building a strong and sustainable organization.

Nurturing a board of directors is

hard work and needs thought and intention. For a board to be effective, it needs to be nurtured and cultivated. The board chair should work to identify ways of ensuring that each board member is engaged in the work of the organization and that he/she feels needed and appreciated. It is also essential to plan board meetings that build the cohesion of the board (the feeling that they are part of a team) and that includes training on issues of importance to the organization and to fulfilling the responsibilities of the board. Board recruitment is an ongoing process and includes the identification of gaps in the board's expertise based on the changing needs of the organization or on who is rotating off of the board.

SUSTAINABLE LEADERSHIP

Typically, when a group or organization breaks down, the dysfunction starts to manifest itself in lack of membership growth and failure to reach goals. Things stop running well, and "group think" can take over, leading to a common negative attitude toward the team or its leaders. Several factors can lead to this dysfunction — including lack of trust, lack of cohesiveness and lack of a clearly defined purpose. Good leadership is the key to positive successful achievements and to sustainability.

"Achievements are not success, sustainability is success."~ Neeraj Kamboj

If you are not learning and growing, you are not standing still, you are going backwards. You can only coast in one direction. Jim Rohn, well known business philosopher and personal development expert, said it so well when he said, "As you become more so you will attract more". The secret to success and realizing your group's full potential is never about pursuing anything, but rather a process of becoming.

When you have an ineffective leader, or one that does not care about the common good of all, things can fall apart quickly. Some successful groups can also suddenly lose their momentum and morale when a new leader takes over. Either group members aren't willing to accept the new team leader, and his or her new way of leading, or the new leader is weak or is more concerned about his or her own agenda.

Building sustainable leadership capacity in any organization is the key.

NARCISSISTIC LEADERS

The more we talk about narcissists, the easier we'll be able to spot -- and avoid -- them!

Narcissus was the handsome man who fell in love with his own reflection. He broke the heart of a mountain nymph named Echo and so the goddess of revenge, Nemesis, lured Narcissus to a pool of water where he saw his own face looking back and became forever depressed that he couldn't have what he wanted.

This kind of self-centeredness is called narcissistic personality disorder, named after the ill-fated Narcissus, and describes an undesirable character who is unfortunately rampant in today's society ... and in the leadership of many people's groups and organizations. With all the pressure on people to succeed in business, in school and in life, it's no wonder that many people 'big' themselves up. Society rewards confidence; it's how you get to the top.

A Psychopath cares little what others think of his or her behavior - while a narcissist puts on a 'public image' of 'perfection' and omnipotence and needs ego support (narcissistic supply). They have no emotions of feelings, little to no empathy or conscience. Avoid- if you must be involved with them set firm boundaries, demand reciprocity, keep them at a distance and expect very little from them. They are toxic personalities that will suck the life out of their targets all the while portraying the illusion of "victim" to their sycophants. They want to be in charge of everything, and have to win little head games.

THINGS REALLY PERSUASIVE PEOPLE DO

Persuasion

Everyone likes to be heard, acknowledged and have their point made. Whether you are trying to persuade a member to remain part of your organization or whether you are trying to convince a prospective member to join your group, persuasion is all about listening.

Most clubs have a goal that is to attract more members to their club, but that's much easier said than done. Effective persuasion is almost like a science that requires one to be patient yet persistent.

Be Purposeful

Persuasion is a skill that needs to be developed. Truly persuasive people recognize and understand their power and use it sparingly and knowingly, when they know they can accomplish what they are going for. Aggressive persuaders are like telemarketers that constantly try to convince you of something to the point where you lose all interest and are turned off by their approach. When you are trying to persuade a member to join your group, you have to be able to defend your arguments. Why should they join? How will they benefit? What can your group offer them? Having a purpose behind your reasons for persuasion can instantly make you more credible.

Listen

Listening is the key to moving the conversation forward. As the person who will be doing the persuading, you already know what your arguments are, and you know why you are persuading the person in front of you. Effective persuasion comes from being able to capitalize on consensus. By listening and focusing on the person in front of you, you are able to gauge how receptive they are to your points and to the subject at hand. By listening for objections, persuasive people are able to make their points more effectively. Finally, by listening for moments of agreements, persuasive people are able to customize their arguments to the person they are convincing.

Create Connections

When you are trying to persuade people to join your club who have no prior connections with your club or its members, it becomes very difficult to convince them. The reason is because it is easy for us to dismiss people when we have no relationship with them or any emotional stake in their argument. In order to be truly persuasive, you have to be listening for those shared objectives and common grounds so you can begin to build a connection and relationship. Connections don't have to be limited to relationships; you can also create connections based on emotions and interests. It isn't necessary for the person you are talking to, to know you or any member of your club - learn more about their interests and form a relationship based on similar interests.

Offer Satisfaction

Patience is a virtue. Persuasive

people understand that their arguments might not lead to a decision today but they know that their goal is to find the easiest path to get that 'yes'. As such, you have to be able to persuade the person in front of you that they will be satisfied upon joining your club. When a person sees how satisfied other members in your club are, their interest level will rise as well.

Acknowledge Credibility

Present them with your club's achievements, past projects and success stories. Present them with how your club has benefited the lives of others. By being able to show your past accomplishments, you are increasing the credibility of your club in the prospects mind and are one step closer in encouraging them to join.

Know when to remain silent and back away

Successful persuasion is not about winning every time. It's one of the reasons why we get so turned off by people who try to convince us of something aggressively. If listening is important, knowing when to be quiet is just as important. Effective persuaders know when they have made their point and when it's time to end the conversation. Every one needs time to think and reflect on the points presented to them. Allow your prospective members some time to think about whether they want to join your group or not, and follow up with them in a few weeks. Urgency and immediacy don't result in the best decisions, so it's important to just make your points and back away. Given time to reflect on your arguments, if made effectively, you can achieve what you set to do.

BEING BORED?

Persistence IS boring! Boring is so essential to getting things done. Building requires real work, some of which is boring, but the growth is exciting... it's an intriguing mix.

Sometimes when we are bored, we have an opportunity to look at the mundane things with new perspective. It may take 'being bored' for looking at being introspective and creative. Being bored is WONDERFUL and FANTASTIC because it gives us a chance to try something new with something old.

"The real story is actually probably pretty boring, right? I mean, we just sat at our computers for six years and coded." -Mark Zuckerberg

No one wants to hear the boring parts, but they're there. Always. People reveal their boring once they've 'made it.' Then boring becomes an intriguing part of the story. Before that, it's just, well... boring.

THE TEST OF THREE

If you practice the 'Test of Three', you will find yourself to be a better leader, and your community to be a better place. When you feel the need to add to the rumor mill or when you are the subject of the rumor mill, remember the 'Test of Three.'

In ancient Greece (469-399 BC), Socrates was widely lauded for his wisdom. One day the great philosopher came upon an acquaintance who ran up to him excitedly and said, "Socrates, do you know what I just heard about one of your students?"

"Wait a moment," Socrates replied. "Before you tell me I'd like you to pass a little test. It's called the Test of Three."

"Test of Three?"

"That's right," Socrates continued. "Before you talk to me about my student let's take a moment to test what you're going to say. The first test is Truth. Have you made absolutely sure that what you are about to tell me is true?"

No," the man said, "actually I just heard about It."

"All right," said Socrates. "So you don't really know if it's true or not.

Now let's try the second test, the test of Goodness. Is what you are about to tell me about my student something good?"

"No, on the contrary…"

"So," Socrates continued, "you want to tell me something bad about him even though you're not certain it's true?"

The man shrugged, a little embarrassed.

Socrates continued. "You may still pass though, because there is a third test – the filter of Usefulness. Is what you want to tell me about my student going to be useful to me?"

"No, not really."

"Well," concluded Socrates, "if

what you want to tell me is neither True nor Good nor even Useful, why tell it to me at all?"

LEADERS ACTIONS SPEAK MORE THAN WORDS

Actions speak louder than words. Leaders who are known for having trust and integrity must **demonstrate** trust and integrity in their relationships.

In my opinion, the key component for a leader or someone to be known for having integrity and trust is **honesty**. To be known by others for being honest, having **integrity** and **trust**, a person needs to demonstrate personal courage; the leader needs to create an environment that is open and transparent; and, you the leader will need to build a strong sense of teamwork and cooperation.

Integrity is often equated with courage- courage to speak up when your point of view is at odds with another person's perspective or with a commonly held belief about how things should be done. Integrity may also be interpreted as work ethic- in early, staying late to get the right things done for the group or organization.

Honesty may be seen as transparency and openness- your willingness to communicate what you're thinking or feeling, even when it is uncomfortable or unpopular. Honesty may be seen as a willingness to listen and discuss issues before the data is completely thought through, when available alternatives are not fully crystallized, and when decisions are not yet final. It may also be seen as keeping your word, following through on promises, and delivering on time.

Trust may be based on a feeling that you have the other person's back when he or she is not in the room. It may be the confidence you will advocate the other person's point of view with clarity and understanding. Or, trust may be gained as you're seen to act in the best interest of the team or organization rather than acting primarily to advance your personal agenda.

ERRORS OF LEADERSHIP

Leadership skills come primarily from experience and common sense. Most people learn best by doing and by learning from mistakes. Great leaders are always willing to take a calculated risk and learn from their mistakes.

By studying leadership behaviors of those they respect and admire, as well as reading thoughts and concepts that other leaders put to paper, it is possible to for folks to make fewer mistakes and continue to grow into the leaders they would like to become.

It is important for leaders to realize that it takes the entire team to take an organization from just good to great. As Jim Collins put it in his book 'Good to Great', leaders have to get the right people on the bus and in the right seats.

LEADERSHIP VERSUS LEADING

There can be a distinct difference between leadership and leading – and some may show great potential for the former but then fail when applied to the latter. It can be easy to talk about leadership in the theoretical sense – what qualities and traits make a good leader, which styles are appropriate – but it is in the actual practice of leadership that many people fall down.

Naturally, different personalities (both of the leader and the followers) and different circumstances call for different ways to do things – however, there are certain steps to keep in mind which can help a person not only show leadership but also actually lead.

1) Have A Strong Vision And Communicate It

A good leader must first personally develop a vision for the group, business or organization and this vision must support the group or organization's goals. Thus knowing the mission of an organization is essential in determining a leader's vision. Once this vision has been formed, it must be described in general terms and then communicated to the team, who then themselves develop the specific objectives and resources required to achieve this vision.

2) Establish Clear Goals

Without goals, progress is slow, inefficient and often misdirected. Therefore, establishing clear goals is an important part of leading. This should be done with the active participation of the rest of the team and while they should reflect the overall vision (described above), they can be more focused and specific. One example of a goal is: "the organization must reduce transportation costs".

3) Determine And Assign The Tasks

In order to accomplish the objectives, specific tasks must be determined and assigned to the appropriate team members with the right skill sets and experience to tackle them. Again, like objectives, tasks are concrete and measurable. Continuing the example from above, an example of a task would be: "The transportation coordinator will obtain detailed shipping rates from at least 10 motor carriers."

4) Set Up A Timeline, Prioritize and Objectives

In order to maximize efficiency, it is important to establish a priority for the tasks to be done, especially as many tasks require others to be completed in a chain before them, before they can be started. Time is valuable and establishing priorities helps to determine the order of tasks and their relative important in accomplishing the objectives. And example of a timeline, in the situation outlined above, would be: "The shipping rates will be obtained by May 9".

Definable objectives are a clear way to provide a measure of progress and the organization's movement towards achievement of the overall vision. It is essentially the strategy for turning a vision into reality. Objectives should be defined in precise measurable terms. Continuing the example from above (No.2) – an example of an objective would be: "by the end of the next quarter, the shipping department will use one parcel service for shipping items under 100 pounds and one motor carrier for shipping items over a hundred pounds."

5) Follow-up, Check And Measure

Once the project has been set in motion, it is a good leader's responsibility to follow-up and measure progress and to check that the team is doing what is required of them. This also demonstrates the leader's commitment in seeing a project through to a successful conclusion.

Effective Leaders Supervise

Good supervision involves keeping a grasp on the situation to ensure that plans and strategies are implemented properly. This can be done via giving clear instructions and inspecting the accomplishments of different tasks. However, it is important to remember that following-up and supervising does not mean "micro-managing". A leader who micro-manages places no trust in others and this can lead to resentment, lowered morale and motivation as well as stifling initative and creativity.

While many people can claim to be leaders, there are fewer who can claim to being "effective leaders" – someone who engenders trust, confidence and respect; who can communicate a vision and inspire others and most importantly, who can make others want to follow him/her and influence the course of their actions – someone who "makes things happen".

Obviously, everyone has different ideas and beliefs about what skills and traits an effective leader should have – for example, if your group values "trust" highly, then it is important that you are viewed as trustworthy by your group in order to be an effective leader.

While some people may be born with more of natural abilities and skills which facilitate the above, effective leadership CAN be learned and leadership potential CAN be developed in every individual. In fact, you don't even have to be officially designated the leader of a group to be an "effective leader".

Here are some of the components most believe to be essential to effective leadership:

• **Communication** – good communications skills does not just relate to speaking ability, although a powerful orator can achieve a lot and lead simply by expressing themselves clearly and with confidence; in fact many famous leaders had brilliant oratory skills. However, good communication skills also involve the ability to listen – and to listen not only to facts but also to feelings. Successful leaders ask and pay attention.

· **Knowledge & Understanding** – an effective leader will understand his organization or group and especially the purpose of the group (why it exists), the goals or long-term plans and its objectives or short-term plans.

- **Team Work** – good leadership involves knowing how to build a team because a leader cannot achieve success alone. In fact, a leader is not at the top of the pyramid, as is often commonly believed, but involved and in touch with group members at every level. Effective leaders think in terms of "we" and not "I".

- **Recognition and Encouragement** – closely linked to team-building is the taking the time and making the effort to recognize and reward group members for their contributions. This helps to inspire and motivate the group, especially when the goal you are aiming for is challenging. Effective leadership is showing a genuine concern, interest and respect for your team members.

· **Vision** – an effective leader not only develops a clear vision of the group's future but is also able to communicate this vision to the members within the group, as well as allowing them to respond and contribute to the visioning process. Vision should be a collaborative effort in the best circumstances – this will produce more commitment and ownership from the team members within the group.

· **Risk and Innovation** – effective leaders have to be willing to take risks and to be open to new ideas and innovations, whether these come from yourself or from others within the group. In fact, a good leader should recognize valuable ideas and actively support and encourage them, even if this involves an element of risk and challenge.

• **Ethics** – to gain the respect of others, a good leader must be ethical and have a clear sense of morals.

• **Flexibility with leadership styles** – an effective leader will also make use of different leadership styles depending on the situation and the group members involved – and the goals to be achieved. A good leader will assess a situation and use an appropriate leadership style or combination of styles.

- **Commitment** – a good leader gives to the group and in doing so, inspires others by example.

IT IS ALL ABOUT HEART

The leader's quality comes from within.

Extreme leadership is an action verb, not a label. It's about doing, not talking. Lots of posers out there, wearing the leadership label. The real leaders are just getting it done.

You can't lead if you can't be audacious enough to think you can change the world. It's not about your ego, it's about having a passion and commitment deep enough that you just can't stop trying. No matter how big the obstacles.

Extreme leadership is risky business. You have to be willing to be the first one to admit you're scared, be willing to put a spotlight on your own failings and mistakes, to have those terrifying moments as you stand at the edge of a cliff and decide to leap.

You're never done: No matter how good of a leader you think you are...there's plenty of room for better. Probably way more than you think, by the way.

There's nothing magical about leadership. It's all in the heart. Anyone can do it, if they care enough. It has to start with heart.

You can't fake it. You can't buy it.

The legacy of a leader is more leaders. The ultimate of leading is to identify those people who you can help and actually lift up so they can be greater than you.

HARASSMENT

Many folks that frequent attending events or conventions have began to ask if there is a harassment policy in place.

If there is a harassment policy, is it clear on what is unacceptable behavior, as well as to whom those who feel harassed, or see others engaging in harassing behavior, can go for help and action?

If there is policy, has the policy: (1) been posted on their Website; (2) placed in their written and electronic programs; (3) put up on flyers in the common areas; (4) being discussed at opening ceremonies?

If there is a policy, are all harassment complaints dealt with promptly and fairly, with no excuses or rationalizations for delaying action when such becomes necessary?

The stated benefits are to address:

· those that see nothing wrong with being a racist and/or sexist and/or homophobe, who attack and harasses people because they feel they have a right to.

· who goes out of their way to make the place uncomfortable and even threatening.

· that having robust, visible and enforced harassment policies go a long way to making these assholes behave, or making them go home.

Living Leadership

LEADING AND COMMUNICATION

For the most part, I believe that all human beings have the best of intentions. Most of us don't go about our days seeking to hurt people with words or actions. We all need a 'rantspace' sometimes. Whether it is to blow off steam at a friend, a colleague, or a group of people whose actions drive us up the wall, we will all whine, moan, and insult just to keep ourselves sane. First of all, there's a difference between using your own experience as a foundation for understanding, and making something about you.

Sometimes this is perpetuated in part by the silence of people when someone does something questionable. The road to understanding is one full of trial and error. What works in one situation may not work in another, and we may be clueless as to why. What is acceptable in society, may not actually be appropriate. I tend to not waste my time on arrogant people. But, I do strive to learn to listen rather than speak. I do strive to pay attention to what they say about their issues, lives, and oppressions.

Contrary to what society teaches us, all relationships – from a conversation between strangers to one with a person that we share an interest – are partnerships. It's a word we throw around a lot, but often our actions may be that we don't really know what it means. It may help to think about it this way: both partners have to continually earn, and reaffirm, that they deserve to be part of the relationship by treating the other person properly, communicating their needs and desires, and acknowledging the right of the other person to have the final say in what they do with their own minds, time or bodies.

There are seven deadly sins that will hamper the leaders success in communication. These are the things that a leader must avoid.

1) Gossip
2) Judging
3) Negativity
4) Complaining
5) Excuses
6) Lying
7) Dogmatism

There are things that a leader should do when communicating. These are to speak with: Honesty, Authenticity, Integrity, and Respect.

ON BEING A LEADER

Today being a leader means demonstrating:

Confidence: Believe in yourself, not only that you can do what you set out to do, but that you already are what you need to be (even if on the outside it doesn't yet show.)

Courage: A leader is courageous (I'm not talking about being willing to do stupid stunts, either), willing to do what is necessary without showing weakness (even if you are scared to death.) A leader cannot be truly courageous and brave if they do not fear something.

Responsibility: Take responsibility for what happens in your life and stop being a victim. Being a victim is exactly what society expects you to be. Be who you really are intended to be – a leader and victor. Make plans and carry them out. Don't fear failure.

Discipline: Take charge of your life and what goes on in it. Carry out and complete your goals. Do everything you say you will do. Eat right and stay in shape, therefore you will also be able to think more clearly.

Honesty, Integrity, and Kindness:

Be honest with yourself and others holding yourself to the highest of standards. Find the fine line between kindness and honesty when necessary. Sometimes, one is more important than the other. With some finesse, you will be able to be honest and kind at the same time. Be kind and gentle toward others, children, and the elderly.

Real leaders treat others with respect and dignity.

Listen: We have two ears and one mouth for good reason – we are supposed to be doing twice as much listening as speaking. When someone speaks, listen with your heart. Instead of thinking, "Oh great, here they go again." think, "They have a need. What is it? What can I do to help." This goes against the nature of people, it seems. They want to strike back and have forgotten who they are dealing with. When someone lets you know they are upset, what they are really doing is asking you to take charge and help. It is a cry for help. Most of the time they just need your love, understanding, and a listening ear. But under no circumstances are you to take abuse from them. Make that very clear. You must keep your cool. No one will not respect a leader who looses their cool.

Defend the Weak: Protect and

provide for your family and anyone who is being unfairly attacked. Be prepared for disasters and have a plan. Refuse to allow anyone to overstep their boundaries, but be smart about how you accomplish this. Plan ahead. Remember, you are a leader so act like one.

Inspire: A leader will always inspire and never force submission.

The key words that I would use to describe the traits of leader today are:

· Freedom
· Direction
· Logic
· Focus
· Integrity

- Stability
- Passion
- Independence
- Discipline
- Confidence
- Aware
- Authentic

IDEAS ABOUT LEADERSHIP

We all have the opportunity to be leaders each and every day or we have the opportunity to chose to follow a leader.

When thinking about leadership, it may be easier to first think about what it is not rather than to try to define it. The prevalence of myths concerning leadership often interferes with both our understanding of leadership and our ability to become better leaders.

One leadership myth stated by

leadership guru Warren G. Bennis is that: *"The most dangerous leadership myth is that leaders are born – that there is a genetic factor to leadership. This myth asserts that people simply either have certain charismatic qualities or not. That's nonsense; in fact, the opposite is true. Leaders are made rather than born."*

Leadership skills and attributes can be taught and learned. Good leadership skills are not developed instantly and it requires a genuine interest and effort to improve leadership skills.

The second myth is that leadership is about possessing power and/or authority over others.

Leadership does involve some form of power or authority. It is important to understand that leadership is not about having power over people nor does it have to involve a formal form of authority. Rather, it is a power **with people** that exists as a reciprocal relationship between a leader and their followers. A good leader will not use manipulation, coercion, and domination to influence others. Leaders who seek group consent and strive to act in the best interests of others are extremely effective.

Peter Drucker says this about leadership: *"Leadership is not magnetic personality – that can just as well be a glib tongue. It is not 'making friends and influencing people' – that is flattery. Leadership is lifting a person's vision to higher sights, the raising of a person's performance to a higher standard, the building of a personality beyond its normal limitations."*

When thinking about leadership, it is important to think about what leadership means. There are many different ideas about leadership.

Leadership means:

· Being willing to guide in the trenches then in an office or miles away from the battle.

· Being willing to take investment

with volunteers because without them, the task wouldn't get done.

· Being willing to take responsibility of one's actions as you would want others to do the same.

· Being willing to listen as much as you speak, to re-examine motivations, and to continue to keep yourself in check with the responsibility of leadership.

· Being strong yet gentle as in the old Japanese ways. Remember being a leader does to mean be a dictator. The masses will revolt.

· Making the tough decisions and seeing them through to fruition.

· Leadership is primarily about

service. Many people who are in leadership roles forget this. They spend all their time trying to prove that they are leaders, usually by trying to dominate their organizations and groups.

· You are a Leader when you quite trying to prove you are a Leader and just be a leader.

· Leadership is taking responsibility and often taking charge.

· It means finding out what those you are trying to lead really want. Then doing everything to help them achieve what they want, not what the leader may want or think is best for them.

· It is incumbent upon the leader to understand and to help each individual within their group to achieve their needs as best as possible.

· To lead you must first be able to follow, to be humble, to have a sense of humility about you.

· To lead you need to have a positive attitude, courage of conviction and unflinching integrity, responsibility and accountability to yourself and those you lead.

· To lead means that you stand up for what is right not what is necessarily easy. Leaders uphold their principles and beliefs and stand by those that they are leading through the good, the bad, and the ugly.

· A leader is one who is in service to their community and the community follows them.

· 'Lead by example.' If you can't back up what you say by your actions, you may call yourself a leader, but no one will follow.

· Leadership is defined in a quote from Star trek: DS9 when Kahless said, *"Great men do not seek power. They have power thrust upon them."*

· Leadership has been described as the *"process of social influence in which one person can enlist the aid and support of others in the accomplishment of a common task".*

(Wikipedia)

· Never forget there is the opportunity to not follow a leader.

· Leadership is being able to ask the hard question and to really listen to the answers no matter if the leader likes them or not.

LEARNING FROM MISTAKES

As John Wooden once said, "If you're not making mistakes, then you're not doing anything."

Mistakes are the pathway to great ideas and innovation. Mistakes are the stepping stones to moving outside the comfort zone to the growing zone where new discoveries are made and great lessons are learned. Mistakes are not failures, they are simply the process of eliminating ways that won't work in order to come closer to the ways that will.

The steps to correcting mistakes apply to any area of life. Whether it's business life or home life or personal life, the principles of apologizing remain the same.

The Six A's of a Proper Apology:

Admit – I made a mistake.

Apologize – I am sorry for making the mistake.

Acknowledge – I recognize where I went wrong that caused my mistake to occur.

Attest – I plan to do the following to fix the mistake on this specific timeline.

Assure – I will put the following

protections in place to ensure that I do not make the same mistake again.

Abstain – Never repeat that same mistake twice.

People who implement the Six A's will find that the level of trust and respect others have for them will grow tenfold. People who implement the Six A's will find that others will be quicker to forgive them and more likely to extend a second chance. It's not the making of a mistake that is generally the problem; it's what you do with it afterward that really counts.

Living Leadership

MENTORING LEADERS

Mentoring is often a buzzword in business, industry, schools, faith based entities and other communities but do we all mean the same thing when we talk about "mentoring leaders"? The terms, "mentor" and "mentoring" are used rather loosely to describe a wide range of roles and activities, and so the words have come to mean different things to different people. I actually find it humorous that this language debate pertaining to the concept of mentoring is frequent worldwide..

Dictionaries can only help us understand what mentoring means. Look up the word, "mentor", and you will most likely find that each dictionary has a slightly different definition. Generally the definitions contain two common elements:

· Trust: The mentor is a trusted individual

· Experience: The mentor is more experienced than the protégé and freely shares that experience with the protégé.

Now look at your thesaurus, and you will find that a mentor can also be thought of as a:

- Friend
- Advisor
- Coach
- Guide
- Teacher
- Role model

The origin of the word 'Mentor' can also be useful in defining mentoring. Greek Mythology holds the history of the word 'Mentor'. Odysseus, the hero of Homer's Iliad, left home to fight in the Trojan War. Odysseus had a son, Telemachus. While Odysseus was off at war, the goddess of domestic arts, Athena, disguised herself as an old man, and became Telemachus' guardian and teacher. Her name was "Mentor".

The modern use of the term mentoring more likely comes from the work of 18th century French writer Fenelon who was also an educator. In addition, African scholars have noted that mentors were commonplace in Africa, long before the ancient Greek civilization.

Leaving the 'wordsmithing' aside there is truly no hard and fast definition for mentoring that is supported by all. Generally it means pairing a learner with someone more senior and more experienced to offer support, encouragement and guidance. The key to mentoring is developing a one-to-one relationship with a goal of strengthening personal development.

A mentor should be someone you can confide in, and ask for help in resolving a situation or making a decision. While mentoring should not be confused with coaching, counseling or training, it can contain an element of all these. A mentor is someone who acts as a role model, compatriot, challenger, guide or cheerleader.

Mentoring, no matter in what segment of society is it being practiced, is the balancing heart, mind and spirit.

FUNDS GONE?

How did someone not notice this happening?

Another instance of funds allegedly misapplied and missing from an organization. Another in a list of disappointments. I have to ask why appropriate financial review and auditing isn't a standard with all organizations dealing with money. It isn't about trust, it's about proper business practices. This is happening too often.

Solid financial business policies

keep people honest even in desperate times. At some level, the Board of Directors must be held accountable for this breach of community trust. Many Board members of organizations do not have a basic understanding of their role. It behooves board members to exercise care in making decisions and providing proper oversight. While it should be *transparency and accountability* in organizations, unfortunately it's *coverup* and something that many prefer is not talked about when a problem occurs.

There does not seem to be adequate oversight in many organizations. It's a combination of not doing proper due diligence in making sure people who are in positions of fiduciary and fiscal responsibility should be (*ex*: are they qualified), and then assuring that the proper safeguards are in place. This is why any organization with more than a couple thousand dollars in the bank should have its officers bonded, and conduct audits at least annually.

Four things I can say with a fair degree of certainty about many nonprofits:

(1) organizations require two people to count each donation and sign checks;

(2) organizations ensure that the person who receives the donations and

records them is not the person who deposits them;

(3) organizations have transparent treasurer's reports with genuine board oversight with monthly reconciliation of the financial records to bank statements by someone other than the Treasurer; and

(4) organizations benefit from employing professional bookkeepers who can educate about expected standards and practices and have a responsibility to point out fraud.

It would seem that organizations sometimes allow one person to hold too many positions and to exercise too much control at the same time. It is not reasonable that any organization's Board of Directors would allow one person to hold the position of Chairman of the Board or President while at the same time being the organization's bookkeeper.

RISKY, DANGEROUS WORK

For all its passion and promise, for all its excitement and rewards, leading can be risky, dangerous work.

Leadership – the kind that surfaces conflict, challenges long-held beliefs, and demands new ways of doing things – causes pain. And when people feel threatened, they take aim at the person leading or pushing for change.

As a result, leaders often get hurt personally and even professionally.

The Paradoxical Commandments
by Dr. Kent M. Keith

People are illogical, unreasonable,
and self-centered.
Love them anyway.

If you do good, people will accuse
you of selfish ulterior motives.
Do good anyway.

If you are successful, you win false
friends and true enemies.
Succeed anyway.

The good you do today will be
forgotten tomorrow.

Do good anyway.

Honesty and frankness make you vulnerable.

Be honest and frank anyway.

The biggest men and women with the biggest ideas can be shot down by the smallest men and women with the smallest minds.

Think big anyway.

People favor underdogs but follow only top dogs.

Fight for a few underdogs anyway.

What you spend years building may be destroyed overnight.

Build anyway.

*People really need help but may
attack you if you do help them.
Help people anyway.*

*Give the world the best you have and
you'll get kicked in the teeth.
Give the world the best you have
anyway.*

Let's change this as leaders to be
rewarding by thinking in a positive
manner.

· People are logical, reasonable and
compassionate.

· If you do good, people will

applaud you.

· If you are successful, you will join the company of other successful people.

· The good you do today will become your legacy.

· Honesty and frankness make you vulnerable and it generates trust which is valuable.

· People with big ideas push the envelope of possibilities and that is worthwhile even if their big ideas get shot down ... temporarily.

· People favor underdogs because it feels good and gives them hope for their own success and there's nothing wrong with following the top dogs for the same reason.

· Destruction is a natural precedent of construction. Consider forest fires.

· People resist change because they are afraid of an unknown alternative. Good leaders know this and alleviate the fear before making the change.

· Giving your best is always appropriate and seldom rewarded poorly.

ENGAGEMENT

Engagement is a measure of a member's attachment to the organization and to their colleagues.

Engaged members are enthusiastic about their work and act in a way that furthers their organization's interests. They perform at consistently high levels, they create stronger relationships, they are less likely to be involved in a safety incident, and are less likely to leave the organization. They are also more likely to suggest or develop creative ideas to improve organizational processes.

Two-way feedback, trust in leadership, shared decision making, an emphasis on member development, and an understanding on the part of group members of how they fit into the big picture and what they must do to help the organization succeed are distinguishing characteristics of an engaged organization.

An engaged membership is essential to a group's continued success. By voicing your opinions about your organization, and your role, you are enabling your organization to substantiate the good work being done and identify the areas of opportunity to promote productivity, retention, and morale.

Living Leadership

AVOIDING POLITICS

Leaders must be aware of specific political tactics and strategies. There are many factors that contribute to organizational politics. Some individual and organizational factors that contribute to political behavior include:

(1) disagreements that prevent rational decision making

(2) emotional insecurity

(3) environmental uncertainty and turbulence

(4) subjective standards of performance

(5) pyramid-shaped organization structure

(6) political behavior in organizations.

You cannot avoid politics in any organization. But you can promote a functional and constructive organizational structure that is effective and productive towards the goals of said organization.

Authentic Principled Leadership is a means to promote functional and constructive relationships within an organizational group.

Emotional containment:. Often

what we talk about has significant emotional values to people and it's very important to be aware of these emotions but speak with rationality on the issues. Recognize and acknowledge people's emotions on a disagreement but keep pointing back to the rational points.

Consistency of action is critical to have credibility in my view. Ones actions need to be consistent over time. Consistency allows people to build trust in them since they are predictable and known to others.

Transparent open mindedness:. Secrets and a closed mind are sure ways to create drama and emotional mud in an organization. A leaders needs to be transparent with is views and ideas be balanced with an open mind to listen to other points of view. Some view leadership being as needed to be a steel rod of determination on ones views. An oak tree can bend with the wind and still be strong as giving more value to an organization.

Considerate decision-making: Much of what occurs in an organization is of a subjective nature and at times leaders must make decisions in these situations. It is important that such decisions are completed with thorough consideration of the various points of view. People need to feel their view point has been heard and understood prior to decisions being made. It is an accepted fact that not everyone will be happy with every decision. But everyone will be happy with the process to the decision if they feel heard and understood.

Even when you choose not to make things personal, others will do so. It is amazing how many people who are emotionally damaged find their way into positions of leadership of organizations and then proceed to make their personal issues a matter for the organization to have to deal with. Alliances form, not because they are best for the organization but easier for the parties involved and all who don't toe the line may find themselves on the wrong side of the fence. Even if one tries not to play the game one will find that there are others who do so and do it well and so you end up either dealing with them or going somewhere else.

Tips:

1. Ensure that the bylaws are consistent with the purpose, organizational structure, and ensures transitional narrative for the group.

2. Ensure the business taken up by the group is the business of the group versus the business of individual members – too many

groups lose sight of their charter.

3. Ensure that the purpose of the group is clear to the membership

4. Ensure the ability of the membership to speak clearly to all points – allowing the amount to time required for redress without filibuster of the group's mission

5. Ensure the business decisions (including the financial statements) are completely transparent to the membership – and, if it is a 501C sort of group gathering donations as well, to the public at large.

6. Ensure a regular transition of power from one person to another in a staggered fashion – and, that this transition is covered under the

bylaws and that it occurs as required.

7. Address concerns quickly, completely and publicly – where the leadership is ignorant of the issue or the solution – state so and ask for assistance in developing a strategy.

8. Forgive minor transgressions easily – punish repeated ones or egregious ones quickly and openly with consensus.

9. If someone offers to quit – accept their terms without hesitation.

10. Take as long as you need to make the important decisions – make the smaller one quickly, decisively and efficiently.

11. Negotiate the best deals possible,

and accept your decision and the word of others as accepted.

12. Avoid battles of will – if you cannot make your point then you do not have one.

13. Listen to others talk with an open mind, if their purpose advances the group and meets the purpose of the organization – back off and support it. Keep your ego under control and remember that ideas are not inherently bad. Misapplication or misdirection is.

Gen. George Patton said, "If everybody is thinking alike, them someone isn't thinking." Yet, we are often *taught* to go along to get along and to take the path of least resistance. You will often hear, "But this is how we've always done things."

In order to survive all things must evolve. Sometimes things must devolve to evolve. Sometimes people must bump heads to make progress. Sometimes a cancer has to be cut away in order for the body to survive. And sometimes it is so pervasive that death is inevitable.

LESSONS FOR LEADERS

1. To thine own self be true.
2. All leaders are passionate about their beliefs, even the ones you don't like.
3. Trust your gut after you have listened, studied and learned from those with a diverse range of opinions.
4. You never know who is watching, so work as hard as you can regardless of the assignment.
5. Don't stay in your comfort zone too long.

6. As my grandmother would say: put yourself in the path of lightning.

7. Be flexible because opportunities rarely knock at the most opportune moments.

8. Take time to be kind to everyone.

9. Focus on your priorities.

10. In order to lead, someone must follow.

11. Effective leadership depends on your ability to connect and motivate people, not on your title, position or power.

12. Set high standards for yourself and your team (lead by example).

13. Take the time to develop personal relationships all along the way, and really cultivate those upon

whom you depend. In order for them to help you, they must know you. And you must know what will motivate them. Nurture them so they can help you lead. They must believe in not just your ideas, but you.

14. Good will matters.

15. Women are particularly good at listening and studying their audience.

16. Have the courage to make tough decisions.

17. When you lead, not everyone will follow, and that's okay.

18. You will fail. Don't take your failures or your success too seriously. Learn to laugh at yourself.

Trust me. It helps.

19. Affiliate yourself with worthy institutions, lead by good people who share your core values.

20. You can have it all, just not at the same time, and in the proportions you may want.

21. To those who much is given, much is expected.

HAVING FUN

People perform best at any task when they're having **fun**. Being relaxed, intent on what they're doing and more or less oblivious of everything else are key ingredients to having fun.

Loosen up and enjoy your life!

Below are a few simple truths to enjoy life more.

1. Don't worry what others will think about you.

2. Stop hiding who you really are.

3. Start being intensely selfish.

4. Stop following the rules.

5. Start scaring yourself.

6. Stop taking it all so seriously.

7. Start getting rid of the crap.

8. Stop being busy.

9. Start something.

PRIVILEGE AND LEADERSHIP

Leading others is a privilege that is earned, not a right.

The privilege of leadership is something to be treasured. Be grateful for the opportunity and pro-actively focused on the service aspect of leadership.

One of the fundamental requirements of a leader is to stay curious. Stay experimental. It is to declare that entropy will not occur on our watch.

With this privilege comes responsibility. A responsibility to challenge our boundaries, stretch and grow. Things that don't evolve, adapt, move ahead become extinct.

Privilege should lead to responsibility. My motto is to *lead by example*.

Diversity and privilege affect interactions within organizations and those they serve. There is an importance for empathy, nonjudgmental attitudes and respect for collaboration across differences.

Managing privilege is a key to inclusive leadership.

CHRISTIAN LEADERSHIP

A little information about Christian Leadership:

In the Bible there are two kinds of leaders represented. There is Satan who represents worldly or evil leadership. And there is Jesus Christ who represents Godly or good leadership. The characteristics of Satan are the opposite of the characteristics of Jesus Christ.

Some of the characteristics and traits of Satan are Arrogance, Dishonesty, Deception, Violence,

Hatred, Self Righteousness, Seeking Lustful Pleasures, Being Materialistic, Being Inconsiderate, Greed, Idolatry, Quarreling, Jealousy, Envy, Selfish Ambition, Outbursts Of Anger, Desire To Rule, Desire Worldly Status, Seeking Praise from People, Attention Seeking, Targeting Feelings and Emotions, Sexual Immorality, Lack Of Self Control, Pride, and Disobedience to God.

Some of the characteristics and traits of Jesus Christ are Holiness, Faith, Hope, Love, Humility, Peace, Honesty, Self Control, Compassion, Patience, Dependable, Goodness, Kindness, Gentleness, Joy, Wisdom, Desire To Serve People, Desire To

Please and Serve God, and Obedience to God.

When it comes to Leadership remember this one thing. In Christ leaders are humble servants. Beware of people who look down on you, view you, think of you or address you as one of their followers. If a Christian leader considers you a follower of them, this is a sign they are not in Christ. In the Bible the leaders chosen by God did not desire followers or a leadership position. And they always encouraged people to follow God. Wanting followers is a characteristic of Satan. It was Satan's desire to be a leader among others that led to his rebellion against God. Instead of wanting angels to follow, worship and praise God. Satan desired the worship and praise of the angels for himself. In the same way Satan also desires people on earth to follow, worship and praise him. This is why Jesus said in the book of Mark,

Mark 10: 42-45 "You know that in this world kings are tyrants and officials lord over the people beneath them. But, among you it should be quite different. Whoever wants to be a leader among you must be your servant and whoever wants to be first must be the slave of all. For even I the Son of Man, came here not to be

126

served, but to serve others and to give my life as a ransom for many."

Beware of people who have a desire to lead; but do not have a desire to serve. That is the opposite of what Jesus Christ taught. If a Christian leader is not willing to serve others he or she is not in Christ. Before you can lead others you must first serve and obey God and allow The Lord Jesus Christ to lead you.

Faith ...Hope...Love

LEADERSHIP TRAINING

If a someone wants to learn about leadership, why not just read John Maxwell's "The 21 Irrefutable Laws of Leadership", Stephen Covey's "Principle-Centered Leadership", or "On Becoming a Leader" by Warren Bennis? Or perhaps just read my book "Shades of Leadership"? Why not go to the nearest major metropolitan convention center and sign up for the next leadership development seminar? Certainly, if one reads those books and attends those seminars, one will learn something about leadership.

Carl Jung said, *'The true leader is always led'* . . . . Authentic leaders know that on their own they are not, and cannot ever be, the compass for the journey; instead they must become a kind of satellite navigational system through which the Universe transmits appropriate directions.

3C'S OF LEADERSHIP

Lou Holtz, the famous football coach and now an analyst on ESPN said there are three questions everyone asks about a leader.

- Can I trust him?

- Does he know what he's talking about?

- Does he care about me?

This can be restated as: character, competency and compassion.

If you don't trust your leader, life's going to be hard. You're parsing everything they say. Looking for discrepancies. Questioning their motives. Thinking "just how many lies does this person think they can tell me without me seeing through them?" There are few leaders we trust completely, but it's awesome to be a part of it when we do. If you can't trust your leader, start looking for other options.

But even trustworthy leaders have to be able to perform. To hold up their end of the bargain. Competency is the easiest of these 3 "C's" to change. Training and experience will likely make this one better over time.

And no matter how trustworthy or

competent, we have to know our leader cares about us. If they don't care, and if we don't know they care, we'll *second guess* their competency or character when something goes wrong.

If you're struggling with your leader, ask these three questions.

BENEFITS FOR SERVING ON A BOARD

There are plenty extrinsic and intrinsic benefits to serving on a nonprofit board.

10. They know their skills are needed.
9. A nonprofit is going to improve and will benefit from their contributions.
8. There is a possibility to effect change in an organization.
7. They will feel good by doing good.
6. They enjoy collaborating with

interesting people who have the

same interests

and values.

5. They want to learn new skills.

4. They enjoy being recognized for

their efforts.

3. They want to give back to the

community.

2. They want to have an impact.

1. It can be fun.

MENTORING LEADERS

Formal, supervised mentoring programs such as youth/adult organizations, school based educational mentoring and company employee programs have a structured intake process for both mentors and protégés. Usually an intake form is completed: a very similar format to a job application. On the form the respective party gives personal and demographic information plus usually answers a variety of questions about expectations, wants, needs and preferences. The intake process usually also includes background and reference checks, criminal record investigation and liability insurance acceptance, Then it is a matter of shuffling forms to match prospective mentors with protégées. Actually, there is a bit more involved with the process but the nutshell version works well for this example.

The process may not be as vigorous and might not be facilitated by a third party but an established format of information exchange would allow for more compatible and successful mentoring relationships. Even if two people have already discussed becoming involved in a formal mentoring relationship it would be beneficial for the two to separately develop written preferences for the liaison. The two may think, from talking and emailing, that the mentoring opportunities are workable between them but closer examination may prove otherwise.

Some concepts one might wish to contemplate when considering searching for a mentor or a protégé.

1. What type of mentoring relationship do you want?

· Educational Mentoring: Directly or indirectly aimed at teaching or improving some specific scholastic information or skill.

· Personal Development Mentoring: Supports the protégé during a stressful or critical developmental period of their life.

· Cultural Based Mentoring: Shares with the protégé the values, customs and practices of a particular culture, faith, group or tradition.

2. What life experiences do you find desirable for a mentor/protégé?

3. What age person would you prefer? Why?

4. What gender person would you prefer? Why?

Some people advocate only same

gender but this doesn't have to be the case. Even national youth mentoring programs now mix genders.

5. What type of person will you not accept in a mentoring relationship? ie: someone in a committed relationship, bigot, straight, gay, etc.

6. Do you want to meet in person on a regularly scheduled basis? If so, how often?

7. Do you want to give/receive written and/or research assignments?

8. What are your goals for entering a mentoring relationship? (general and specific)

The key is to have a quality
mentoring relationship, one that
produces significant, lasting,
positive outcomes for protégées.
Quality mentoring is responsible,
ethical and usually effective.

ADULT BULLYING ...
IT CAN HAPPEN TO YOU

You may not hear a lot about adult bullying, but it is a problem. It is important to learn more about different types of adult bullies and get some ideas on how to deal with an adult bully. Adult bullying is a serious problem and may require legal action.

One would think that as people mature and progress through life, that they would stop behaviors of their youth. Unfortunately, this is not always the case. Sadly, adults can be bullies, just as children and teenagers can be bullies. While adults are more likely to use verbal bullying as opposed to physical bullying, the fact of the matter is that adult bullying exists. The goal of an adult bully is to gain power over another person, and make himself or herself the dominant adult. They try to humiliate victims, and "show them who is boss." Bullying within organizations happens when a group of people who have a particular agenda will use allegations, obscure rules, and group attacks to silence dissent or minimize the questioning of their activities. In small organizations all one has to do is hint at impropriety and a snowball effect can occur and there are quite a few who are adept at behind the scenes whispering or as the expression goes, "throwing a rock and hiding their hand." This misdirection and casting of aspersions are another form of bullying.

There are several different types of adult bullies, and it helps to know how they operate:

Narcissistic Adult Bully: This type of adult bully is self-centered and does not share empathy with others. Additionally, there is little anxiety about consequences. He or she seems to feel good about him or herself, but in reality has a brittle narcissism that requires putting others down.

Impulsive Adult Bully: Adult bullies in this category are more spontaneous and plan their bullying out less. Even if consequences are likely, this adult bully has a hard time restraining his or her behavior. In some cases, this type of bullying may be unintentional, resulting in periods of stress, or when the bully is actually upset or concerned about something unconnected with the victim.

Physical Bully: While adult bullying rarely turns to physical confrontation, there are, nonetheless, bullies that use physicality. In some cases, the adult bully may not actually physically harm the victim, but may use the threat of harm, or physical domination through looming. Additionally, a physical bully may damage or steal a victim's property, rather than physically confronting the victim.

Verbal Adult Bully: Words can be quite damaging. Adult bullies who use this type of tactic may start rumors about the victim, or use sarcastic or demeaning language to dominate or humiliate another person. This subtle type of bullying also has the advantage – to the bully – of being difficult to document. However, the emotional and psychological impacts of verbal bullying can be felt quite keenly and can result in reduced job performance and even depression. Secondary Adult Bully: This is someone who does not initiate the bullying, but joins in so that he or she does not actually become a victim down the road. Secondary bullies may feel bad about what they are doing, but are more concerned about protecting themselves.

Workplace bullying can make life quite miserable and difficult.

Supervisors should be made aware of adult bullies, since they can disrupt productivity, create a hostile work environment (opening the company to the risk of a law suit) and reduce morale.

The anonymity of the internet contributes to cyber bullying. There are many people who would not be confrontational face to face that think nothing of making rude, hurtful or incendiary comments via the internet. Usually these are people with aliases, or people who you would never actually run across in physically. They use the Internet as a mask and shield because they lack the temerity to confront someone face to face and the intellect to confront some one in sophisticated dialogue.

It is important to note, though, that there is little you can do about an adult bully, other than ignore and try to avoid, after reporting the abuse to a supervisor. This is because adult bullies are often in a set pattern. They are not interested in working things out and they are not interested in compromise. Rather, adult bullies are more interested in power and domination. They want to feel as though they are important and preferred, and they accomplish this by bringing others down. There is very little you can do to change an adult bully, beyond working within the confines of laws and company regulations that are set up. The good news is that, if you can document the bullying, there are legal and civil remedies for harassment, abuse and other forms of bullying. But you have to be able to document the case.

Adult bullies were often either bullies as children, or bullied as children. Understanding this about them may be able to help you cope with the behavior. But there is little you can do about it beyond doing your best to ignore the bully, report his or her behavior to the proper authorities, and document the instances of bullying so that you can take legal action down the road if necessary.

Dealing with Bullying

Dealing with bullying, or a bully, can be difficult and traumatic for people of any age. If you are a victim of bullying, or fear your child or teen is being bullied, this article is a must read. It contains tips for dealing with a bully and helping understand bullying is not acceptable.

Bullying can be a very traumatic experience. It can cause physical and emotional harm, and damage you for a long time to come. Indeed, a victim of bullying can suffer from physical injury, but the long lasting effects to someone's psyche can be even more damaging in the long term, even though these effects might be subtle. It is also important to note that bullying can take place without physical contact. Emotional, verbal and electronic (online or through text messaging on cell phones) abuse can cause the same emotional and psychological effects as physical bullying. Being bullied can lead to difficulty in forming healthy personal relationships, as well as leading to depression, low self image and even suicide.

The American Academy of Child

and Adolescent Psychiatry bullying statistics estimate that about half of all children are bullied at some point during their school years. Close to 10 percent of children are bullied repeatedly. This is a rather large number, when you think about it. This means that it is vital that your child learns how to deal with bullying.

Tips for dealing with bullying, or a bully

It can be difficult to deal with bullying, or a bully. It is more helpful when a bully's parents, friends, employer, church, school community are involved as well, working to help diffuse the situation. If you are concerned that someone you know is the victim of bullying, here are six steps you can take to try and help him or her in dealing with bullying:

Get input: You need to be in a safe place you can turn for help when dealing with bullying. Be open to your friends, family, and social network, and make sure that they know you dealing with bullying. You should let anyone being bullied know that being bullied is not his or her fault. Also, you should find out what has been tried to stop the bullying, and what has worked (or hasn't worked) so far.

Talk to the

school/employer/authorities:
Discuss the problem. A meeting can
help everyone know how to help,
and who is dealing with bullying. In
many cases, bullying takes place in
unsupervised areas, such as school,
on line, buses, shopping areas,
restaurants, bars, bathrooms, parks,
sports leagues, and other areas that
can be hard to monitor. If you know
where the bullying is taking place,
you can let authorities know so that
they can step up "patrols" are take
actions in those areas to discourage
bullying.

Try to avoid the bully: You do not
need to fight back. Avoid the bully
when possible. Suggest that he or

she walk away.

Be assertive: It is not necessary to fight back to defeat a bully. You can stand up straight and tell the bully, firmly, to leave me/him or her alone. In some cases, this type of assertiveness will work.

Practice: It might be beneficial to have a little bit of role play. This way you can practice what to say to a bully, or how to leave a situation that could turn into bullying.

Move in groups: A good support system can be an effective deterrent against bullies. Go places with trusted and true friends when dealing with bullying.

It is also important to help your family and your friends understand that it is not acceptable to harm others, physically, emotionally, verbally or electronically (cyberbullying). Indeed, you should teach your child to stand up to bullies who may be harasses other children. If your child and his or her friends are willing to come to the aid of others who are being bullied, soon the bully will have no one left to pick on.

Another important aspect of dealing with bullying is to watch your own child/friends/employees for signs that he or she might be a bully. It can be difficult to see such behavior, but you need to take bullying seriously, and let everyone know that it is inappropriate. If know a bully, take the time to find out why he or she may be acting this way. In some cases, a psychologist or developmental expert can help you figure out the reasons behind the behavior and work to change these behaviors.

Bullying can have long lasting effects on people. What happens can set the tone for the rest of one's life, and it is important that bullying is dealt with early on.

Living Leadership

BULLYING ... THE FACTS

The following activity allowed students to explore the problem of bullying through an informal group survey.

Teens were divided into 40 groups and asked to create a survey question related to bullying. Once each group created their question, they spent ten minutes mingling with other groups and collecting responses to their group question. Students were instructed to note which groups' questions they'd already answered to ensure their responses would not be replicated in the same group's data. Each group was able to survey at least 25% of the 400 students present, though each group's pool of respondents was unique, depending on whom they mingled with during the ten-minute timeframe.

After collecting responses, students returned to their small groups and compiled their statistics. Though many groups asked the same question, responses varied based on how their version of the question was worded, and on the specific pool of students they surveyed.

The purpose of this informal survey was to allow teens to share their experience and perspectives on bullying and promote dialogue. After reporting and discussing the results with the large group, student returned to their small groups to brainstorm ways to address bullying back at their schools.

Survey Questions and Answers

1. Have you ever reached out to people being bullied? 85.6% Yes 14.4% No

2. Have you ever made an effort to stop bullying? 80% Yes 20% No

3. Have you ever stood up for someone being bullied? 80% Yes 20%

No

4. When you see bullying, how often do you intervene? 60% Occasionally 30% Frequently 10% Never

5. When you see bullying, do you ignore it and walk away, report it to someone, or try to stop it? 45% Try to stop it 28% Report it to someone 27% Ignore it and walk away

6. In the past year, have you acted against bullying? 77% Yes 23% No

7. Have you ever witnessed bullying? If yes, did you take action? 95% Yes (60% Take action 40% Did not take action) 5% No

8. When you see bullying, how often do you stop it? 48% Most of the time

36% Rarely 8.5% Always 7.5% Never

9. What do you do when you see someone being bullied? 56.4% Intervene 24.6% Nothing 16.6% Report It 2.4% Go along with it

10. How many times have you witnessed bullying and did not act upon it? 60% 1-3 times 26% 4 or more times 14% Never

11. Have you ever bullied someone? 73% Yes 27% No

12. Have you ever bullied a close friend out of your life? 31% Yes 69% No

13. Have you ever bullied because you were: 67% Joking 17% Bullied Yourself 11% Having a Bad Day 5%

Other

14. For what reason are teenagers bullied the most? 86% Appearance/Body Image 12.8% Race 1.2% Financial Background 0% Religion

15. Is allowing bullying just as bad as the act of bullying? 90.4 Yes 9.6% No

16. At what grade level do you think bullying starts? 66% Elementary School 28% Middle School 6% High School

17. What grades have you been bullied in the most? 50% Middle School 25% Elementary School 25% High School

18. Where do you think bullying is the biggest problem? 51.5% Middle School 35.9% High School 7.7% Elementary School 4.9% Outside of school

19. Where do you think the most bullying takes place? 45% Middle School 40% High School 15% Elementary School 0% After high school

20. Is bullying at your school subtle or obvious? 64% Subtle 36% Obvious

21. How does bullying affect kids psychologically? 56% Depends on kid 33% Makes them insecure 9% Makes them stronger 2% Does not affect them.

22. Is psychological bullying as

damaging as physical bullying? 83% Yes 17% No

23. Do you feel like a bully has permanently damaged you? 63% No 37% Yes

24. How much do you think a person's future is affected by bullying? 83% Significantly 16% Slightly 1% Not at all

25. Who have you turned to in an instance when you were bullied? 28% Friends/Peers 28% No one 12% Family 4% School/Faculty 28% Two or more of the above

26. Which hurts more? 60% Verbal Bullying 40% Cyber Bullying

27. What type of bullying do you see

most at school? 50% Verbal 38%
Cyber 10% Racial 2% Sexual 0%
Physical

28. What type of bullying is most
common in your community? 40%
Cyber 37% Verbal 3% Physical 20%
All of the above

29. What form of bullying do you
see most often? 55% Cyber 45% In
Person

30. What do you consider to be the
most common type of bullying? 60%
Cyber 39% Verbal 1% Physical

31. Of the bullying that you witness,
is the majority cyber bullying or
physical bullying? 69% Cyber
bullying 31% Physical bullying

32. What is the most severe form of bullying? 43.4% Mental bullying 4.1% Physical bullying 52.5% Both

33. Which type of bullying is more predominant at your school? 62% Cyber 38% Physical/Verbal

34. Which is more serious, confrontation bullying or cyber bullying? 56% Confrontational 44% Cyber

35. Which form of bullying is most prominent at your school? 49% Verbal 42% Cyber 9% Physical

36. What is the most prominent form of bullying that you see at your school? 48% Verbal/mental 42% Cyber 10% Physical

37. Where do you see bullying most?
61% Internet 35% School 2% Home
2% Other

38. Who bullies you the most in your
life? 42 % Peers 18% Friends 14%
Family 2% Teachers/Other Leaders
24% None of the above – not bullied

39. Have you ever changed your
daily routine to avoid bullying? 52%
Yes 48% No

40. Is bullying as bad as the media
makes it seem? 42% Accurate and
not helping 24% Accurate and
helping 18% Inaccurate and helping
14% Inaccurate and not helping

POWER IN LEADERSHIP

All kinds of power are useful and valid as long as it's the right kind for the task. Leaders do not always get to decide what kind of power they have in an organization. You don't have to be in a leadership or senior level role in an organization to have some form of power. In fact, the most respect is garnered on those who have personal sources of power. There is more respect for these individuals than for those who have power simply because they are the boss.

Successful leaders tends to focus on getting the job done and developing the team, as opposed to how he can misuse his positional power to advance personal gains. That's why leaders that are not too interested in being powerful tend to end up with better reputations.

Equating power with personal success is kind of a cultural and social phenomenon; it's not universal but it is certainly common.

It has been shown that when others in an organization associate the leadership's power with expert or referent power, they are more engaged, more devoted to the organization and their role within it. They are also more willing to go the extra mile to reach organizational goals.

Power means many different things to different people. For some, power is of no interest at all. For others, the more power they have, the more successful they feel. For even others, power is seen as corrupt.

The five bases of power were identified by John French and Bertram Raven in the early 1960's through a study they had conducted on power in leadership roles. The study showed how different types of power affected one's leadership ability and success in a leadership role.

The five bases of power are divided in two categories:

Formal Power

Coercive

Coercive power is conveyed through fear of losing one's job, being demoted, receiving a poor performance review, having prime projects taken away, etc. This power is gotten through threatening others. An example is the Membership Director who threatens everyone to meet their goals or get replaced.

Reward

Reward power is conveyed through rewarding individuals for compliance with one's wishes. This may be done through giving bonuses, raises, a promotion, extra time off from work, etc. For example, the supervisor who provides employees comp time when they meet an objective set for a project.

Legitimate

Legitimate power comes from having a position of power in an organization, such as being the boss or a key member of a leadership team. This power comes when employees in the organization recognize the authority of the position. For example, the CEO who determines the overall direction of the organization and its resource needs.

Personal Power

Expert

Expert power comes from one's experiences, skills or knowledge. As we gain experience in particular areas, and become thought leaders in those areas, we begin to gather expert power that can be utilized to get others to help us meet our goals. For example, the Project Manager who is an expert at solving particularly challenging problems to ensure a project stays on track.

Referent

Referent power comes from being trusted and respected. We can gain referent power when others trust what we do and respect us for how we handle situations. For example, the member known for ensuring that others are treated fairly and coming to the rescue of those who are not

CREDIBILITY AS A LEADER

Your credibility is based on your words and actions. If these two areas of communication are incongruent, your credibility will suffer. So if you are a team member and tell your teammates you will help out but never do, your credibility will diminish as a result.

Whether you're sharing information or job recognition, if you are not credible, it will be of little consequence. If you expect others to believe what you say, you first have to believe it yourself.

According to the *American Heritage Dictionary*, credible means: "1. Capable of being believed; plausible. 2. Worthy of confidence; reliable." Credibility is how believable you are to others.

James Kouzes, author of *Credibility: How Leaders Gain and Lose It, Why People Demand It*, says, "Credibility is the foundation of leadership. If people don't believe in the messenger, they won't believe the message." In business, if you lack credibility, you may never be able to get a team to follow you and will probably never advance to a position of authority. Let's face it:

If people don't believe what you say, nothing else really matters.

No matter who you are or where you are within your organization, you must build credibility and steer clear of all that will destroy it. Consider this your number one priority and promise yourself you will never get caught in a situation that forces you to compromise your credibility.

To maintain credibility every leader and potential leader needs to avoid these mistakes.

1. **Not Accepting Personal Responsibility:** If you're not willing

to accept personal responsibility for what you do, then you will lose credibility. Others will perceive you as fake or a self-serving jerk. "Leaders, whether in the boardroom or on the front line, are at the center of a vast web of relationships," Kouzes says. "Leaders must reach out and attend to all their constituents if they wish to be credible... credibility, like quality and service, is determined by the constituents, so leaders must be able to view themselves as their constituents do."

2. Not Telling the Truth: Lying to your staff and customers or fellow club members or employees is always a terrible idea. "Leaders and those aspiring to be leaders must recognize that self-serving behavior is the trail to organizational suicide," Kouzes says. Be honest with others, and you will better serve yourself and your organization in the long run.

3. Withholding Information: Good leaders and team members do not keep information from others. When you withhold information, it is perceived as being controlling at best, lying at worst.

4. Failing to Keep Up with Your Field of Expertise: No matter what you do, there are almost always changes. And if you don't stay abreast of the advances, others will see you as a weak leader. People want to follow leaders who are current, knowledgeable and confident. If you don't know your field, your credibility suffers, because you're no longer believable.

5. Trying to Get People to Like You Rather Than Respect You: Typically, a person who is trying to be liked rather than respected is perceived as insincere, phony and noncredible. Building likeability is no more than being a glad-hander. These people run into meetings all smiles and try to shake hands with everyone, but they are not the least bit interested in anyone and are interested only in their own agendas.

MAINTAINING MOMENTUM

It is the leader's responsibility to keep the ball rolling, utilizing and maintaining momentum to not just achieve immediate objectives, but your long-term vision as well. Unfortunately, just because forward motion is being made, it is not guaranteed to stay. If momentum starts fading, there is a tendency for others, and even you as the leader, to find yourselves going through the motions of complacency. Therefore, not only must momentum be created, but a premium should be placed on making it last.

When good leaders see momentum developing within their organization and harness it, positive results happen at a much more rapid pace and success becomes almost second nature. But to keep momentum going, you must revisit what started it, re-set goals, and re-energize, recognize and reward your team.

In the sports world, momentum is everything, and can change in the blink of an eye, swinging quickly from one direction to another. As Baseball Hall of Fame Baltimore Orioles Manager Earl Weaver once observed, "Momentum is the next day's starting pitcher."

In the professional world, momentum is perhaps not as fickle, but it is no less important. To have great success, momentum must be created. Casting a new vision, setting initiatives in place, the creation of a team, and a series of successes are all ways in which momentum can be built. And when a leader recognizes that momentum is occurring, and takes full advantage of it, the results can be outstanding.

Review Individual Efforts

"Individual commitment to a

group effort—that is what makes a team work, a company work, a society work, a civilization work," Super Bowl-winning coach Vince Lombardi once said. Individual efforts within your organization helped create the initial momentum, and they will be crucial to helping maintain it.

In addition to establishing new goals, meet individually with each player on your team. Evaluate their contributions for the previous momentum push and outline the next steps needed from him or her to keep things accelerating. Also gauge their perspective of where things were, where they are now and where they are going to keep an active read on the momentum pulse of your corporate culture.

Remind

Something started the momentum you are experiencing. While you may not be able to completely recapture what created the initial buzz, you can facilitate events that will remind your team of what got them here.

Holding outings, retreats, training sessions, rallies and team-building exercises on a regular basis will rekindle the original vision and purpose of the team, helping further a sense of excitement and keep your pace.

Re-Set Greater Challenges

Perhaps the easiest thing to do to maintain momentum for your team is to keep raising the bar. Once a goal is achieved, it is easy for your organization as a whole to ease off the accelerator, pull back and catch a collective breath. Simon & Schuster publishing icon Michael Korda offered this advice: "One way to keep momentum going is to have constantly greater goals."

Setting new objectives each time one is achieved will consistently keep you moving full steam ahead corporately. Keep the new goals attainable and in line with what got you started—and make sure they fit in with the overall vision you have already created.

Recognize and Reward

Being a part of something big can get anyone excited and build momentum. But once the newness is gone, catering to the individual can keep things rolling for your team. Celebrate victories that have been hard-earned to generate the momentum by rewarding your team, either with symbolic accolades or real value awards.

Offer ongoing incentives for team members who routinely go above and beyond and recognize their efforts on an organizational-wide basis. Not only will it encourage recipients to continue their efforts, but others will be motivated as well.

Re-Energize

You do not want to be a task master, constantly pushing people to the brink of exhaustion, to keep momentum. Create a break when appropriate to prevent burn out—whether it is an outing or simply a day away from the routine—allowing everyone to get re-energized and refocused on the task at hand. Keep the focus on re-energizing, not relaxing.

MY DEFINITION OF LEADERSHIP

My definition of "leadership" is being able to: inspire others, motivate, set a vision, communicate, respect others, and lead by example. A leader must have an honest understanding of who they are, what they know, and what they are capable of doing. To be successful you have to convince others who may choose to follow you (not yourself or your superiors) that you are worthy of being followed. In my opinion this can build confidence in others and their faith in you to be able to lead.

Being a leader you will encounter different situations. What you do in one situation will not always work in another. In different scenarios I have used good judgment to decide the best course of action needed for a situation. For example, a person may need to confront a group member for inappropriate behavior, but if the confrontation is too late or too early, too harsh or too weak, then the results may prove ineffective. For me a person can lead through two-way communication. Much of it is nonverbal. For instance, when you "set the example," that communicates to other people that you would not ask them to perform anything that you would not be willing to do.

How I communicate either builds or can harm the relationship between my peers and myself. In order to achieve a goal, a leader must take charge and assign different people certain tasks. Also, leadership of a group can mean a way of having a more strategic plan when overcoming an obstacle. A person can build stronger character within themselves in showing leadership to others. In conclusion, it is essential that we continue to build leadership skills, in ourselves and others, because it will be beneficial for our future.

Thomas Smith